The updated # Belgium

Travel guide 2023/2024

Discover the Heart of Europe
Your Ultimate Belgium Travel Companion
2023/2024

LISA ROBERT

This guide is designed for informational purposes only and does not constitute professional advice. While every effort has been made to ensure the accuracy of the information presented, neither the author nor the publisher assumes any responsibility for errors or omissions. Travelers are encouraged to verify information, conduct their own research, and exercise personal discretion when planning their journeys.

CONTENT

PACKING LIST

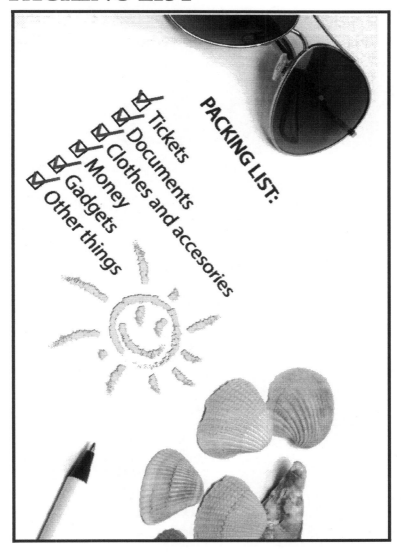

PACKING LIST:

- ☑ Tickets
- ☑ Documents
- ☑ Clothes and accesories
- ☑ Money
- ☑ Gadgets
- ☑ Other things

MAP OF BELGIUM

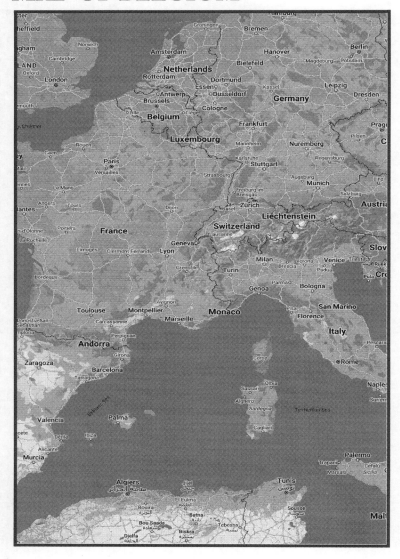

ABOUT THE AUTHOR

Hello, I'm Lisa Robert, the author of this Belgium travel guide. As an ardent traveller and a dedicated writer, I've had the great chance to experience the magnificent landscapes, rich history, and lively culture of this lovely European country. My enthusiasm for adventure and exploration has brought me to various corners of the globe, but Belgium maintains a particular place in my heart.

My path into travel writing began with a strong respect for the stories concealed inside the cobblestone alleyways of Bruges, the ancient elegance of Brussels, the artistic pulse of Antwerp, and the mediaeval beauty of Ghent.

Over the years, I've immersed myself in the distinctive fabric of Belgium's towns, countryside, and coast, diving into its historical treasures, tasting its gastronomic pleasures, and participating in its colourful festivals.

I believe that travel is not only about visiting sites; it's about feeling the soul of a destination. Through this book, I hope to share my experiences and knowledge, providing you with a complete resource that encapsulates the enchantment of Belgium. From practical travel suggestions to historical background, cultural subtleties, and hidden jewels, I've strived to develop a book that lets you enjoy the essence of this wonderful nation.

I'm pleased to be your virtual guide, bringing Belgium to life through the pages of this book. I hope it encourages you to embark on your own trip, experiencing the magnificent landscapes, enjoying excellent cuisine, and immersing yourself in the warmth of Belgian culture. May your tour across Belgium be filled with wonderful experiences and cherished memories.

Bon voyage, and I wish you a fantastic trip in Belgium.

Warm regards,

Lisa Robert

Introduction

Belgium, noted for its delicate lacework of cultures, beautiful landscapes, and tasty chocolates, welcomes you with open arms. This fascinating region, nestled in the heart of Western Europe, may be small in size, but it delivers a powerful punch in terms of history, art, and gastronomic quality. As you prepare to travel to Belgium, allow me to take you on a virtual tour of this enchanting country, revealing what makes it a must-see trip in 2023.

A historical tapestry

Belgium, known as the crossroads of Europe, has a long and illustrious history dating back to Roman times. History is carved into every cobblestone and architectural wonder, from the mediaeval splendour of Bruges to the lively streets of Brussels.

Begin your historical journey in Bruges, a city that has been compared to an open-air museum. The well-preserved mediaeval architecture, such as the famed Belfry of Bruges and the attractive canal system, will transport you to another time and place. As you meander through the cobblestone alleys and enjoy scrumptious Belgian chocolates, you'll see why Bruges is known as the "Venice of the North."

Ghent, another historical treasure, offers an intriguing mix of tradition and modernity. The Ghent Altarpiece, a masterwork by Jan van Eyck, and the magnificent Gravensteen Castle tell of a glorious history. Nonetheless, Ghent's thriving arts scene, student population, and lively festivals bring the city to life.

Antwerp, a bustling international centre, is the birthplace of renowned artist Peter Paul Rubens. The Rubenshuis, his former home, is now a museum displaying his masterpieces. The Grote Markt, the city's historic core, is a sight to behold, especially in the evening when the buildings are illuminated, creating a magnificent ambience.

The world-famous Atomium, a spectacular portrayal of an iron crystal amplified 165 billion times, may be found in Brussels, the nation's capital. It exemplifies Belgium's modernism and scientific prowess. But as you walk through its ancient core, the Grand Place, you'll realise why it's a UNESCO World Heritage Site, a testament to the country's everlasting veneration for its past.

Geographical   Diversity

Belgium is more than simply a historical treasure trove; it is a country endowed with geographical diversity that will take your breath away. Every location conveys a different tale, from the undulating hills of the Ardennes to the lovely Belgian shore.

The Ardennes, located in southern Belgium, is known for its lush forests, flowing rivers, and attractive villages. It's an outdoor enthusiast's dream, with hiking, kayaking, and cycling opportunities. The splendour of this verdant region is obvious in its pristine landscapes, where legends and folklore echo through the years.

The Belgian Coast contrasts sharply with the lush Ardennes. This coastline, which runs along the North Sea, is home to golden sandy beaches, bustling promenades, and lively coastal villages. You'll discover peace by the water's edge while you breathe in the sea air and eat fresh fish.

Excellence in Culinary Arts

Belgium's culinary culture reflects its cultural diversity and appreciation for the finest things in life. Prepare to savour a variety of delightful treats, including world-renowned Belgian chocolates, waffles, beer, and mussels.

Belgian chocolate is a source of pride for the country. The country's artisanal chocolatiers create delectable confections that are as pleasing to the eye as they are to the palate. Discover small chocolate stores and the art of praline manufacturing.

Belgian waffles are a gastronomic wonder in and of themselves. These light and airy desserts are frequently accompanied by a mix of toppings such as whipped cream, fruit, and chocolate sauce. You'll be in culinary heaven as you savour a warm Belgian waffle at a delightful café.

Belgian beer, which is famous all over the world, is more than just a beverage; it is an intrinsic element of Belgian culture. You're in for a tastebud trip with over 2,000 different beer varieties, including Trappist ales, lambics, and saisons. Visit local breweries and beer museums to obtain a better understanding of this national gem.

Belgian mussels, often known as "Moules-frites," are a popular delicacy that you should taste. These plump mussels are commonly served with crispy fries in a delicious soup. It's a traditional Belgian dish that combines the flavour of the sea with a touch of history.

Traditions and festivals

Belgium's calendar is jam-packed with vivid festivals and traditions that provide a glimpse into the country's character. While there are various events throughout the year, the following are some highlights:

The Flower Carpet Festival in Brussels: The Grand Place in Brussels is decked with a spectacular carpet of fresh flowers every two years, producing a mesmerising tapestry of colour and perfume.

Carnival of Binche: This UNESCO-recognised carnival, held in the town of Binche, is a beautiful and unique festival that incorporates

Gilles, who dress up in colourful costumes and toss oranges to the audience as a symbol of good luck.

The Ommegang of Brussels is a spectacular event that features knights, nobility, and stunning costumes. It is a historical reenactment of a 16th-century parade.

Tomorrowland Music Festival: If you like electronic music, Tomorrowland in Belgium is one of the world's most famous music events. It's a captivating fusion of music, art, and dance.

Paradise for Travellers

Belgium provides a seamless travel experience with a well-developed transit system that allows visitors to easily explore the country's different areas. Trains, trams, and buses effectively connect cities and villages, and a network of bike routes allows you to explore the country at your leisure.

Belgium is a multilingual country with three official languages: Dutch, French, and German. English is also commonly spoken, making communication with other travellers simple.

Belgium's lodging options include everything from lovely bed & breakfasts to opulent hotels and cosy hostels. Regardless of your budget or preferences, you'll be able to find a place to call home throughout your visit.

Discover the essence of Belgium

Consider the variety of activities that await you as you prepare to travel to Belgium. This wonderful country combines the old and the new, the historic and the modern, the serene and the vibrant in a harmonic symphony that will stay with you for years.

Your Belgian vacation will be full of contrasts and surprises, from savouring exquisite Belgian chocolates in the shadow of Bruges' mediaeval towers to dancing to electronic beats at Tomorrowland. It's a place where history and tradition collide with innovation and imagination, and where every waffle bite and drink of beer tells a tale.

As you read through the pages of this travel book, you'll discover a wealth of information, suggestions, and recommendations to help you plan a successful trip.

An   Overview   of   Belgium

Belgium, located in the heart of Western Europe, is a country with a rich history, diverse culture, and stunning beauty. Here's a summary of what this interesting nation has to offer:

Belgium is usually described as a cultural crossroads due to its linguistic diversity. The country's three official languages, Dutch, French, and German, reflect its varied identity.

Belgium has a rich historical past, spanning from the mediaeval splendour of Bruges to the opulence of Brussels. The exquisite architecture, museums, and UNESCO World Heritage Sites reflect the country's heritage.

Belgian cuisine is famous for its delectable chocolates, waffles, and beer. Don't miss out on the opportunity to sample these delicious delights in their natural surroundings.

The lush woodlands of the Ardennes to the golden beaches of the North Sea coast are examples of Belgium's natural beauty. Outdoor enthusiasts and wildlife aficionados have various alternatives to explore.

Belgium is famous for its vibrant festivals and customs. Expect to see vibrant parades, historic reenactments, and noisy festivals all year.

What to Look Forward to During Your Vacation

Belgium is a holiday destination with a wide range of activities. If you go, here's what you can expect:

Explore the country's historical sites, museums, and architectural marvels. The ancient cities of Bruges and Ghent will transport you back in time, while Brussels seamlessly blends history and contemporary.

Art & Culture: Belgium has always been a hotbed of creative and cultural innovation. Discover the works of great painters like Jan van Eyck and Rubens, as well as contemporary art scenes in cities like Antwerp.

gourmet Delights: For foodies, Belgian cuisine is a gourmet treat. Explore the vast world of Belgian beer while enjoying world-renowned chocolates and waffles topped with a rainbow of delights.

Exploration of Nature: Whether hiking in the Ardennes, biking along beautiful roads, or resting on the beach, Belgium's natural beauty will captivate you.

Festivals and Celebrations: Participate in the festivities to get into the joyous Belgian atmosphere. The Flower Carpet Festival, Binche Carnival, and Tomorrowland are just a few of the events that showcase Belgium's upbeat personality.

Suggestions and Recommendations for Travel

Consider the following travel tips and ideas as you plan your trip to Belgium to make the most of your adventure:

Visa and entrance Requirements: Check the visa and entrance requirements for your nationality before going. Check that your travel documents are up to date.

Best Time to Visit: Because the weather in Belgium fluctuates, plan your vacation around your interests. Spring and summer are pleasant seasons, while autumn brings gorgeous foliage. The winter season is ideal for visiting Belgian Christmas markets.

Budgeting and Currency: Belgium is a reasonably priced destination. Learn about the Euro currency and exchange rates. Create a budget for housing, food, transportation, and activities.

Belgium has a well-developed and efficient public transport system. Trains, trams, and buses connect cities and communities. Consider purchasing a "OmniCard" or "City Card" for simple travel.

While the official languages are Dutch, French, and German, English is widely spoken, particularly in tourist areas. Learning a few basic Dutch and French phrases may improve your experience.

Belgium offers a wide range of lodging options, from expensive hotels to charming bed and breakfasts and budget-friendly hostels. Plan your hotel ahead of time, especially during peak tourist seasons.

Safety and Health: Belgium is generally a safe place, however basic precautions should be followed. Keep an eye on your belongings, be aware of your surroundings, and use caution when crossing roads.

Belgians are recognised for their courtesy and regard for personal space. Tipping is typical at restaurants, and rounding up the amount is appreciated. Depending on where you are, greeting someone with a handshake or a kiss on the cheek is customary.

Check the weather forecast for the duration of your trip and pack accordingly. It is recommended that you bring good walking shoes, an umbrella, and a varied wardrobe. Bring a power adapter to keep your electronics charged.

Local gastronomy: Approach Belgian gastronomy with an open mind. Moules-frites (mussels with fries) and stoofvlees (beef stew) are popular local meals. Make room for chocolates, waffles, and a wide range of Belgian beers.

Belgium will take you through time, culture, and nature. This lovely nation has something for everyone, whether you're like art, history, gastronomy, or adventure. Discover Belgium's hidden gems, sample its cuisines, and immerse yourself in its rich tapestry of history. Your adventure to Belgium begins right here.

Chapter 1: Discovering Belgium

Belgium, known as the "Heart of Europe," is a region of mystery and discovery. This chapter takes us on a trip to peel back the layers of this enthralling country, beginning with an examination of its rich and convoluted past. Discovering Belgium is similar to flipping the pages of a history book, but it's about more than simply the past; it's about comprehending the historical fabric that has built this magnificent country.

Belgium's Profound History

Belgium's history is rich and intriguing. This small but powerful nation has seen empires rise and fall, mediaeval splendour grow and fall, and the formation of a distinct national identity.

Belgium's history dates back to the Roman Empire, when it was part of the province of Gallia Belgica. Tournai, with its well-preserved Romanesque architecture, bears witness to the Roman impact.

Mediaeval Grandeur: During the mediaeval period, mighty duchies rose to power and awe-inspiring Gothic churches were built. During this period, cities such as Bruges and

Ghent developed, collecting riches and cultural treasures.

Spanish authority: As part of the Habsburg Empire, Belgium came under Spanish authority in the 16th century. Religious strife and Emperor Charles V's famous abdication highlighted this time in history.

The Napoleonic Era: The early nineteenth century saw the reign of Napoleon Bonaparte, who left his imprint on the nation through administrative changes and the establishment of the Kingdom of Holland.

Independence and World Wars: Belgium's route to independence in 1830 was fraught with difficulties. The country was involved in both World Wars, becoming a battlefield in both.

War wounds may still be seen in intact trenches and memorials.

European Union: Following World War II, Belgium was instrumental in the development of the European Union, with Brussels acting as its de facto capital. This shift towards European integration has had a significant influence on Belgian identity.

As you travel across Belgium, you will come across relics of its rich history at every step. The mediaeval belfries, Gothic cathedrals, and ancient battlefields are not simply remnants but live testaments to a nation's perseverance in the face of adversity.

Must-See   Historical   Sites

Grand Place, Brussels: The great plaza of Brussels is an architectural masterpiece, with elaborate guildhalls reflecting the city's mediaeval splendour.

Belgium's belfries are UNESCO World Heritage Sites that represent the country's economic and civic might during the Middle Ages.

Ypres Battlefields: Visiting the Ypres battlefields and cemeteries allows you to pay respect to the sacrifices made during World War I.

Cinquantenaire Park in Brussels holds the Royal Museum of the Armed Forces and Military History and has a triumphal arch designed to commemorate Belgium's 50th anniversary.

The Atomium, Brussels: As a symbol of Belgium's forward-thinking attitude towards science and technology, this landmark structure embodies the spirit of development that has shaped the country.

Belgium's history is a tapestry of stories, achievements, and problems, rather than a collection of facts and dates. Take time to immerse yourself in this amazing country's history, which has left an unmistakable impact on its culture, art, and identity.

Historical   Monuments

Belgium is a historical treasure trove, with each brick and stone telling a tale about the country's past. Here are a handful of the most amazing historical places you should not miss:

The Grand Place in Brussels is a UNESCO World Heritage Site that features a beautiful mix of Gothic and Baroque buildings. The guildhalls' golden façade bears witness to the city's mediaeval splendour.

Belfries of Belgium and France: Belgium has 33 belfries, 23 of which are designated as UNESCO World Heritage Sites. During the Middle Ages, these tall monuments functioned as emblems of the city's riches and authority.

Bruges' Historic Centre: Known as the "Venice of the North," Bruges has an immaculately maintained mediaeval city centre. The picturesque canals, mediaeval houses, and cobblestone alleys take tourists back in time.

Gravensteen Castle in Ghent: A visit to this spectacular mediaeval fortification transports you to the Middle Ages. Learn about its history as you explore its dungeons, battlements, and towers.

Tournai Cathedral: This cathedral, dedicated to Our Lady, is a UNESCO World Heritage Site known for its Romanesque architecture. It is one of Europe's oldest Gothic cathedrals.

Cultural Heritage and Museums

A plethora of museums and cultural organisations showcase Belgium's cultural past. Here are a few must-see museums:

Brussels' Royal Museums of Fine Arts have a vast collection of Belgian and foreign art, including pieces by René Magritte, Pieter Bruegel the Elder, and Hieronymus Bosch.

Antwerp's MAS | Museum aan de Stroom is a modern museum that emphasises the city's nautical heritage and cultural variety. The rooftop offers breathtaking views of Antwerp.

Ghent STAM: The City Museum of Ghent, with interactive exhibitions and multimedia presentations, takes visitors on a compelling trip through the city's history, culture, and people.

Musical Instrument Museum (MIM), Brussels: Housed in an Art Nouveau building, MIM has a remarkable collection of musical instruments from all over the world, making it a one-of-a-kind and harmonic experience.

Autoworld, Brussels: Car aficionados will like this motor museum, which features an excellent collection of classic cars from various eras.

Traditions and festivals

Belgian festivals and customs are strongly ingrained in the country's culture and history. Here are a few noteworthy occasions:

The Flower Carpet Festival, Brussels: Every two years, the Grand Place is transformed into a spectacular carpet of fresh flowers, producing a mesmerising tapestry of colour and aroma.

Binche Carnival: This UNESCO-recognised carnival in Binche has masks, music, and Gilles (colourful characters) who throw oranges to the throng as a symbol of good luck.

The Ommegang of Brussels is a historical reenactment of a 16th-century parade that includes knights, aristocracy, and magnificent costumes.

Tomorrowland Music Event: This world-famous electronic music event, held in Boom, is a fusion of music, art, and dancing. It draws visitors from all around the world.

Geographical Variability

Belgium is a tiny nation, yet it has a great geographical variety. There are a variety of locations to explore, ranging from rolling hills to sandy shores.

Landscapes and regions

Ardennes: The Ardennes, located in the south, is a thickly wooded region with hills, rivers, and lovely villages. It's a refuge for hikers, wildlife lovers, and people looking for a peaceful escape.

The Belgian Coast: With its sandy beaches, bustling promenades, and colourful coastal towns, the Belgian Coast stands out. It's an ideal location for a coastal vacation.

Weather and climate information

Belgians have a moderate coastal climate with warm summers and chilly winters. The optimal time to visit is determined by your own preferences.

Spring (March to May) is ideal for visiting old cities since the weather is warm and gardens are in bloom.

Summer (June through August): Ideal for beach vacations, outdoor activities, and festivals.

Autumn (September to November): A beautiful season for seeing autumn foliage and visiting cultural places.

Winter (December to February): The Ardennes' season for Christmas markets and winter sports Outdoor Recreation

The various landscapes of Belgium provide a wide selection of outdoor activities.

Hiking: Discover the Ardennes' large network of hiking paths, which provide scenic vistas and wildlife interactions.

Cycling: Cycling trails crisscross Belgium, making it a cyclist's heaven.

Kayaking: Because the Belgian Ardennes are famed for their waterways, kayaking and canoeing are popular activities.

During the warmer months, you may enjoy swimming, sunbathing, and water sports along the shore.

Belgium is a country that begs to be explored with its mix of historical treasures, cultural riches, and natural beauty. Whether you're interested in history, art, or the beautiful outdoors, Belgium has something for everyone.

Chapter 2: Trip Planning

In Chapter 2, we look at the practical aspects of organising a trip to Belgium. We attempt to provide you with the important knowledge you need to make your trip seamless and enjoyable, from admission requirements to the ideal time to visit. This section focuses on one of the first stages in planning your trip to Belgium: comprehending the country's visa and admission procedures.

Entry requirements and visas

Before beginning your Belgian vacation, it is important to understand the visa and entrance procedures. The specifics will depend on your nationality, the reason for your travel, and the length of your stay. Consider the following crucial points:

- 1. Belgium is a member of the Schengen Area, a group of European nations that have eliminated passports and other forms of border control at their common borders. If you are a citizen of a Schengen Area member nation, you can visit Belgium without a visa and travel freely across the Schengen Zone.

- 2. Visa Waiver Nations: Belgium, like the other Schengen nations, has visa waiver arrangements with numerous countries, enabling its people to travel without a visa for up to 90 days within a 180-day period for tourist, business, or family reasons. You can enter Belgium without a visa if your country is on the list of visa-waiver nations.

- 3. Visa Requirements: If your country is not on the list of visa waiver nations, you may need to apply for a Schengen visa at your home country's Belgian embassy or consulate. A passport, proof of travel insurance, proof of lodging, and evidence of financial means to sustain your stay are normally required as part of the visa application procedure. Because visa processing dates vary, it is best to apply well in advance of your intended travel.

- 4. Stay Duration: Schengen visas for Belgium typically allow travellers to stay in Belgium and the Schengen Area for up to 90 days within a 180-day period. Overstaying can result in penalties, deportation, or future travel restrictions, so it's critical to stick to the rules.

- 5. Visas for Residency and Job: If you intend to stay in Belgium for reasons other than tourism, such as a job or study, you must apply for the proper resident or work visa. These visas have special conditions, such as job contracts, proof of enrollment in a school, or proof of family reunification.

- 6. Passport Validity: Make sure your passport is valid for at least three months after your anticipated departure date from Belgium. It's also a good idea to keep some blank pages in your passport for arrival and departure stamps.

- 7. Trip papers: Make copies of all vital trip papers, such as your passport, visa (if necessary), travel insurance, and a printed itinerary. Keep digital copies in a safe place online.

- 8. Documentation of Accommodation and Financial Resources: Be prepared to show documentation of your lodging arrangements in Belgium as well as proof of sufficient financial resources to sustain your stay. Bank statements or a letter of sponsorship may be included.

- 9. Extra documents: Depending on your circumstances, you may be required to provide extra documents such as a letter of invitation, a no-objection certificate from your job or educational institution, or confirmation of your links to your home country.

Visa and entrance criteria can be complicated and vary over time, so it's important to check the official website of the Belgian embassy or consulate in your country for the most up-to-date information. Furthermore, it is recommended that you speak with the embassy or consulate to confirm that you have all of the required papers and satisfy the specific criteria for your journey to Belgium.

Understanding and satisfying visa and entrance criteria is an important aspect of arranging your vacation to Belgium, as it assures a smooth and pleasurable experience when you arrive in this beautiful and culturally rich European country.

Travel Records

The cornerstone of each overseas voyage is the travel documents, which ensure your easy entry and stay in Belgium. Here's all you need to know about travel documents:

Passport: Your passport is the most significant travel document you can have. It must be valid for at least three months after your departure date from Belgium. Check your passport's expiration date well in advance and, if necessary, consider renewing it.

Visa: You may require a Schengen visa to enter Belgium, depending on your nationality and the purpose of your visit. Apply for the appropriate visa type (tourist, business, family, etc.). The visa should be requested from your home country's Belgian embassy or consulate.

Travel Insurance: While not a standard travel document, travel insurance is important. It covers unforeseen situations like travel cancellations, medical crises, and misplaced luggage. Examine the insurance to check that it covers your whole trip and that it satisfies the Schengen visa criteria.

Flight Itinerary: You may be required to provide a paper or electronic flight itinerary detailing your admission and exit from Belgium. Check that your flights correspond to the period of your visa.

Proof of Accommodation: You may be required to submit proof of your lodging arrangements in Belgium. Hotel reservations, Airbnb bookings, or a letter of invitation from a host might all be included.

Financial Resources: It is critical to demonstrate that you have the financial resources to finance your stay. If necessary, bring bank statements or a letter of sponsorship.

Prepare an emergency contact list, including the contact details for your country's embassy or consulate in Belgium. Knowing where to go for help in the event of an emergency is critical.

Make copies of all of your trip papers, including your passport, visa, travel insurance, and airline itinerary. Save digital copies at a secure and easily accessible internet location as well.

Visa   Guidelines

Belgium, being a member of the Schengen Area, has a visa system that travellers must follow. Here is some vital information regarding Belgium visas:

Schengen Visa: A Schengen visa is usually required if you want to enter Belgium for tourist, business, or family reasons. It permits you to travel for up to 90 days during a 180-day period inside the Schengen Area.

Visa Waiver Countries: Citizens of some countries, including the United States, Canada, and Australia, do not need a visa to visit Belgium for short periods of time. They may arrive as tourists or for other non-work-related reasons.

If you are not from a visa-free nation, you must apply for a Schengen visa at the Belgian embassy or consulate in your home country. Typically, the application procedure consists of submitting required papers, undergoing an interview, and paying a fee.

Visa processing periods differ based on your location and the time of year. Because processing might take several weeks, it's best to apply well in advance of your scheduled trip.

Schengen Visa Types: Schengen visas are classified into three types: tourist visas, business visas, and family visit visas. Choose the one that matches your trip goal.

Schengen visas are not often extended. If you want to remain longer, you may need to depart the Schengen Area and re-enter after the validity of your visa has expired.

When is the best time to visit?

The ideal time to visit Belgium is determined by your choices and the sort of experience you are looking for.

Spring (**March to May**): Spring is a beautiful season to visit since the weather is mild, flowers blossom, and gardens spring to life. It's perfect for sightseeing in cities and visiting historic places.

Summer (**June–August**): The summer season is ideal for outdoor activities and festivals. The weather is pleasant, and it is the ideal time for outdoor activities, eating, and beach vacations.

Autumn (**September to November**): Autumn is a beautiful season to visit the countryside and cultural attractions because of the brilliant foliage. It's also harvest season, which means great local stuff is in season.

Winter (**December to February**): Winter is the season for Christmas markets and a cosy, festive atmosphere in Belgium. Skiing and snowboarding are available in the Ardennes if you enjoy winter sports.

Consider your desired climate, the sort of activities you want to participate in, and the ambience you want to experience while arranging your vacation. Belgium's allure transcends seasons, with something exceptional to offer at all times of the year.

Seasonal High Points

Belgium's allure changes with the seasons, providing a range of experiences all year. Consider the following seasonal highlights while planning your visit:

From March until May:

Witness the well-known Flower Carpet Festival in Brussels (biannual; the next one is in 2024).

Visit blossoming gardens like Keukenhof in the Netherlands, which is conveniently accessible from Belgium.

Enjoy nice weather for sightseeing and outdoor activities in the city.

Summer months (June through August):

Attend world-famous music events such as Tomorrowland in Boom.

Immerse yourself in the vibrant atmosphere of Belgian coastal towns with crowded promenades.

Enjoy excellent seafood while relaxing on sandy beaches.

The Brussels Summer Festival is a lively festival of music and culture.

From September until November:

Enjoy the vibrant colours of autumn leaves in parks and woodlands.

Participate in local beer festivals and try seasonal beers.

Visit historical places when they are less crowded.

From December until February:

Experience the joyful atmosphere of Christmas markets in Brussels, Bruges, and Ghent.

Skiing and snowboarding are popular winter activities in the Ardennes.

Sip hot chocolate and relax at quaint cafés.

Calendar of Events

Throughout the year, Belgium conducts a variety of events and festivals to celebrate its rich culture, art, and customs. Among the important occurrences are:

The Flower Carpet Festival (**Brussels**): Every two years, the Grand Place in Brussels is decorated with a spectacular carpet of fresh flowers, producing a mesmerising tapestry of colour and aroma.

Binche Carnival (**Binche**): a UNESCO-recognised carnival with colourful masks and Gilles tossing oranges into the throng for good luck.

Ommegang of Brussels (**Brussels**): A historical reenactment of a 16th-century procession, complete with knights, nobles, and spectacular costumes.

Tomorrowland (**Boom**) is one of the world's most well-known electronic music events, with a captivating mix of music, art, and dancing.

Brussels Christmas Market (**Brussels**): A spectacular winter experience complete with festive decorations, ice skating, and seasonal delights

Gentse Feesten (**Ghent**): A lively city-wide festival with music, theatre, street entertainment, and gastronomic treats

Trappist Beer Weekend (**Various Locations**): A celebration of Trappist beers made by monks in several Belgian monasteries

Currency and budgeting

Belgium is regarded as a modestly priced destination. Budgeting and understanding the currency are key to making the most of your trip.

Belgium's official currency is the euro (€). For convenience, it's best to convert some money before your vacation; however, ATMs are widely available for cash withdrawals.

Budget: Your budget will be determined by a variety of criteria, including your travel style, lodging options, and planned activities. A mid-range daily budget for a single traveller might range from **€80** to **€150** on average.

Accommodation costs vary greatly depending on location and kind. Hostels and economy hotels are less expensive, but luxury lodgings are more expensive. Consider making a reservation in advance, especially during busy tourist seasons.

Food: Depending on the establishment, dining out might be inexpensive or lavish. Sampling local dishes at smaller, family-run establishments may be both tasty and cost-effective.

Belgium has a well-developed public transit system. Train travel is a practical and inexpensive way to see the nation. For discounts and convenience, consider acquiring an "OmniCard" or "City Card."

Keep in mind the admission prices to museums, historic sites, and attractions. Many cities offer tourist cards that allow you to visit many sites for a single fee.

Belgium is well-known for its chocolates, beer, and lace. Make room in your budget for some souvenir purchases.

Tipping is commonly done at restaurants, and it is typical to round up the cost. A service charge may already be incorporated in some circumstances.

When planning your vacation to Belgium, keep your specific interests and priorities in mind. While exploring on a budget is conceivable, there are also several options for indulgence and exquisite experiences in this charming European city.

Currency Conversion

Belgium's currency exchange is simple because the Euro (€) is the country's official currency. Here's what you should know about currency exchange in Belgium:

The Euro is split into seven banknotes and eight coins, with notes ranging from €5 to €500 and coins ranging from 1 cent to 2 euros. To manage transactions more easily, become acquainted with the various currencies.

ATMs are widely distributed across Belgium, including in smaller towns and villages. They provide an easy option to withdraw euros in local currencies. For international acceptance, make sure your debit or credit card bears the Visa or MasterCard logo.

Currency exchange offices: While they may be found in large cities and tourist locations, they frequently charge greater fees and offer less favourable conversion rates than ATMs. Withdrawing money from ATMs is often less expensive.

Credit and debit cards are commonly accepted across Belgium, particularly in metropolitan areas. To avoid card holds for suspicious purchases, notify your bank of your vacation intentions.

Traveller's checks are becoming less popular as ATMs and credit cards become more prevalent. If you choose this option, you must swap them at a bank or a currency exchange agency.

Banks: Belgian banks are the most dependable locations to exchange cash. They have reasonable pricing; however, their hours of operation may be limited. When exchanging money at a bank, always be sure to provide valid identification.

The euro's exchange rate varies against other currencies on a daily basis. Before exchanging money or completing transactions, it's a good idea to check the most recent rates online or using a currency converter app.

The Cost of Living

Belgium's cost of living ranges from modest to high, with costs varying by area and city. The following is an overview of the cost of living in Belgium:

Accommodation: The cost of lodging is affected by location and kind. Smaller towns tend to be less expensive than Brussels and other large cities. Hostels, cheap hotels, and Airbnb rentals are less expensive choices, but luxury hotels are more expensive.

Dining: Depending on the establishment, eating out in Belgium can range from inexpensive to upmarket. Street food, neighbourhood brasseries, and tiny family-run eateries provide affordable alternatives. Of course, fine dining and gourmet restaurants will be more expensive.

Transportation: Belgium offers a well-developed public transportation system, with reasonably priced train and tram tickets for visiting the nation. Consider transit cards such as the "OmniCard" or "City Card," which may save visitors money.

Groceries: Supermarkets and local markets provide a variety of low-cost self-catering choices. A broad variety of items are available, including high-quality chocolates, cheeses, and local beers.

Entrance costs for museums, attractions, and cultural events might vary. Many cities sell tourist cards that grant admission to various sites for a single charge, possibly saving travellers money.

Utilities: If you're staying in long-term housing, you may be required to pay for utilities such as power, water, and internet. These prices vary, but they are often reasonable.

Belgium is famous for its chocolates, beer, and lace. Souvenir pricing might vary, so it's a good idea to research prices across stores to discover the best offers.

Tipping is traditional at restaurants and is usually around 10% of the total cost. A service charge may already be included in the bill in some areas.

While Belgium may be a modestly priced vacation, there are ways to save costs and experience the country on a budget. Balance your expenditures and enjoy a variety of local activities, from street food to cultural events, to make your trip to Belgium more affordable.

Chapter 3: Getting Around Belgium

In Chapter 3, we'll look at how to move around and see Belgium. It is simple to do thanks to the country's efficient and well-connected transportation network. Here, we'll look at the many kinds of transit available to help you go from one Belgian jewel to the next.

Belgium provides a varied range of transit alternatives, making it simple for visitors to see its cities, villages, and picturesque countryside. Here are the main types of travel in Belgium to help you get around:

Trains: The Belgian railway system is large, effectively linking cities, towns, and regions. Trains are well-known for their reliability and comfort. The rail network is operated by the

Belgian Rail Company (**SNCB/NMBS**), and you may check timetables and purchase tickets online. For cheap rail travel, consider the **"OmniCard" or "City Card**."

Trams and buses: Trams and buses give quick access to places that trains do not immediately service. They are well integrated into public transit, giving you the freedom to explore smaller towns and rural regions. Tram and bus tickets are frequently interchangeable.

Metro: Both Brussels and Antwerp have metro systems that are quite useful for moving around the cities and getting to significant sites. The Metro in Brussels is also an easy way to get to the European Quarter and the city's international institutions.

Taxis: Taxis are plentiful in cities and tourist locations. They are more expensive than public transit, but they might be a practical choice for shorter distances or when travelling in a group.

Car Rentals: Renting a car is an excellent alternative if you want to explore the Belgian countryside or visit inaccessible locations. Major vehicle rental companies have locations at airports and major centres. Keep in mind that Belgians drive on the left side of the road.

Cycling: Belgium is a biker's paradise, with several dedicated bike tracks and lanes. Many cities hire bikes, allowing you to explore places at your own leisure. Cycling is a fantastic way to appreciate the natural beauty of rural areas such as the Ardennes.

Walking: The layouts of Belgium's cities and towns are noted for being pedestrian-friendly. Walking is an excellent method to see ancient city centres, as well as a peaceful and ecologically responsible approach to learning about the local culture.

Transportation Cards and Passes

Consider utilising transit passes and cards to make your trip more easy and cost-effective.

OmniCard: The OmniCard, which is available in several cities, provides unlimited travel on trams, buses, and metros within a particular area. It's a low-cost way to get around cities.

City Card: Many cities give tourist cards that provide free or reduced entry to main sites and public transit. These cards might help you save money and streamline your travel arrangements.

Rail Pass: If you want to travel extensively by train, consider purchasing a Rail Pass, which permits you unlimited train rides over a specified time period. It's ideal for visiting numerous cities and areas.

Additional Tips for Getting Around Belgium

Use the Belgian Rail App: The SNCB/NMBS app is an excellent resource for checking train timetables and purchasing tickets on the fly.

Purchase Advance Tickets: Purchasing your transit tickets ahead of time might save you time and money. This is very beneficial for train rides.

Schedules should be checked. Transportation timetables sometimes change, so make sure to check the most up-to-date information before your trip.

Cards for Public Transportation: Contactless cards for public transit are available in several locations, including Brussels and Antwerp. These cards make commuting easier and may be refilled as needed.

Bike Rentals: Use city bike rental services to explore metropolitan regions or picturesque countryside routes.

The superb transport network in Belgium guarantees that you can simply explore the nation and access all of the sights on your agenda. Whether you prefer trains, trams, buses, or a combination of modes of transportation, Belgium's transportation alternatives are intended to improve your travel experience.

Transportation by Public

Belgium has an efficient and well-connected public transit system that makes exploring cities, villages, and regions a breeze. Here's everything you need to know about Belgian public transport:

Trains: The Belgian train system is well-known for its timeliness and comfort. The bulk of rail services are operated by the Belgian Rail Company (SNCB/NMBS). Trains are a great way to travel between cities since they have regular connections.

Trams and buses: Trams and buses are essential for getting around cities, small towns, and rural locations that aren't served by railroads. They are incorporated into the public transit network, providing flexibility and coverage.

Metro: Both Brussels and Antwerp have metro systems that make it easy to navigate inside the cities. The Metro in Brussels is extremely handy for getting to the European Quarter and crucial institutions.

Tickets and cards are available at train stations, online, and via vending machines. For limitless travel inside certain locations, consider using transit passes or city cards. For convenience, several cities provide contactless public transit cards.

Timetables and Route Maps: Timetables and route maps are readily accessible and simple to use. They include timetables, routes, and stop information. Mobile applications are also useful for checking real-time data.

Driving Hints

Here are some important driving recommendations if you want to drive in Belgium:

Belgians drive on the right side of the road, with the driver's seat on the vehicle's left side.

Road Signs: Learn about Belgian road signs and traffic rules. Signs are usually written in both Dutch and French.

Parking might be difficult to find in urban centres. Look for parking lots or garages, and be prepared to pay for parking in big cities.

Speed restrictions: Pay attention to speed restrictions, which differ based on the kind of road. It's usually 50 km/h (31 mph) in cities, although roads allow up to 120 km/h (75 mph).

Roundabouts: There are several roundabouts in Belgium. Follow the right-of-way laws and yield to vehicles inside the circle.

Drunk Driving: Belgium has strong drunk driving regulations. Because the legal blood alcohol level is low, it is best not to drink and drive.

Seat Belts: All passengers in the car must use seat belts.

Tolls: Toll roads exist in Belgium, mostly on motorways. Be prepared to pay tolls or, for added convenience, consider getting a prepaid toll card (e.g., Viapass).

Cycling and walking

Belgium is well-known for its walkable cities and well-kept bike routes. Here are some riding and walking suggestions for Belgium:

Cycling: Belgium is a cyclist's paradise, with dedicated bike tracks and lanes. Many cities provide bike rentals, allowing you to explore places at your leisure. Cycling is a great way to see the landscape in rural areas like the Ardennes.

Walking: The historic centres of Belgium's cities and towns are attractive and ideal for touring on foot. Cobblestone streets and pedestrian zones encourage leisurely strolls that allow you to immerse yourself in the local culture.

Follow traffic laws and keep vigilant when cycling. Make sure your bicycle has lights for night riding. Use marked crosswalks and heed traffic signals when walking.

Communication and language

Belgium has three official languages: Dutch, French, and German. Here's how to deal with language diversity:

Dutch is the major language in Flanders' northern area. Even though many Flemish people know English, learning a few simple Dutch words might be useful.

French is the predominant language in Wallonia's southern portion and in Brussels. Although English is commonly spoken at tourist-oriented restaurants, knowing French is advantageous in these places.

German is spoken in a tiny area in the east, near the German border. Because English is not widely spoken in this region, some knowledge of German may be advantageous.

English is commonly spoken, particularly in cities, among the younger population, and in the tourism sector. The majority of the signage and information are also available in English.

Communication: Belgians are typically kind and accommodating. When approaching locals, begin a discussion with a warm hello in the local tongue.

Belgium's linguistic variety contributes to its cultural diversity. While English is sufficient in most situations, making an effort to utilise local languages or grasp cultural subtleties may enrich your experience and interactions with Belgians.

An Overview of the Language

One of Belgium's distinguishing traits is its linguistic variety. The official languages of the nation are Dutch, French, and German. Here is a list of the languages spoken in various regions:

Dutch: The most frequently spoken language in Belgium, Dutch is also the official language of the Flemish Region in the north. The majority of Belgians in Flanders speak Dutch, including Antwerp, Ghent, and Bruges.

French is the official language of the southern Walloon Region and the Brussels-Capital Region. French is the predominant language in places like Brussels, Liège, and Namur.

German: A tiny German-speaking community may be found in eastern Belgium, close to the

German border. This region's official language is German.

English is commonly spoken, especially in cities, among the younger population, and in the tourism business. The majority of Belgians, particularly in cities, speak English well.

Useful Expressions

While many Belgians speak English, learning a few simple words in the local languages may be beneficial and enrich your vacation experience.

Here are some handy Dutch and French phrases:

Dutch (Flemish):

Hello - Hallo (HAH-loh)

Please - Alsjeblieft (AHL-syuh-bleeft)

Thank you - Dank je wel (DAHNGK yuh vayl)

Yes - Ja (yah)

No - Nee (nay)

Excuse me - Pardon (pahr-DOHN)

I don't understand - Ik begrijp het niet (ik buh-HRAYP hut neet)

How much does this cost? - Hoeveel kost dit? (HUH-vayl kost dit?)

Where is the restroom? - Waar is het toilet? (waar is hut TOY-let?)

Goodbye - Tot ziens (tot zeens)

French:

Hello - Bonjour (bohn-ZHOOR)

Please - S'il vous plaît (seel voo pleh)

Thank you - Merci (mehr-SEE)

Yes - Oui (wee)

No - Non (noh)

Excuse me - Excusez-moi (ehk-SKEW-zay mwah)

I don't understand - Je ne comprends pas (zhuh nuh kohm-PRAHNG pah)

How much does this cost? - Combien ça coûte ? (kohm-byen sah koot?)

Where is the restroom? - Où sont les toilettes ? (oo sohn lay twah-LET?)

Goodbye - Au revoir (oh ruh-VWAHR)

Alternatives for Accommodation

Belgium has a variety of hotel alternatives to meet a variety of budgets and interests. Here are some popular options:

Hotels: Belgium boasts a variety of hotels, ranging from low-cost to high-end alternatives.

There are well-known multinational chains as well as beautiful boutique hotels.

Hostels: Hostels are perfect for budget-conscious travellers, as they provide both dormitory-style and private rooms. They frequently provide community spaces for socialising.

Bed and breakfasts (B&Bs): B&Bs provide a comfortable and personalised stay in local homes. They are widespread in rural regions and provide a sense of Belgian friendliness.

Apartments and Airbnb: Renting apartments or utilising Airbnb might be an excellent choice for families or travellers looking for more room and the chance to prepare their own meals.

Camping: Belgium has a variety of campgrounds in attractive areas such as the Ardennes and along the coast. Camping is a common activity among nature lovers.

Châteaux and Boutique Hotels: For a truly unique experience, try staying in a château or boutique hotel. Belgium has several lovely old homes that have been converted into luxurious hotels.

Budget Accommodations: Belgium also has a variety of low-cost choices, such as guesthouses and budget hotels. These are common in most cities and towns.

Regardless of your lodging preference, it is best to reserve ahead of time, especially during busy tourist seasons. The sort of lodging you choose depends on your travel style and interests, so when in Belgium, look into the possibilities that best fit your needs.

Hotels

Hotels in Belgium cater to a wide spectrum of travellers, from those looking for low-cost hotels to those looking for premium accommodations. Here's what you can anticipate from Belgian hotels:

Budget Hotels: Budget hotels abound in Belgium, particularly in metropolitan areas. These hotels provide clean, basic rooms and minimal facilities, making them suitable for budget-conscious travellers.

Hotels in the Mid-Range: Mid-range hotels in Belgium are pleasant and well-equipped. They frequently provide facilities like Wi-Fi, TV, and en-suite bathrooms. Many are affiliated with well-known multinational companies or local boutique businesses.

Luxury Hotels: Belgium has a plethora of luxury hotels, many of which are built in ancient houses or châteaux. These hotels provide luxurious rooms, gourmet meals, spa services, and superb service. A stay at a luxury hotel in a city like Brussels or Bruges may be an extravagant experience.

Business Hotels: Major Belgian towns such as Brussels and Antwerp have business-oriented hotels with sophisticated conference facilities and convenient access to corporate centres.

Old and Boutique Hotels: Because Belgium has a rich history, several old structures have been converted into boutique hotels. Staying at one of these institutions provides a unique and immersive experience.

Amenities: Most Belgian hotels have complimentary Wi-Fi, flat-screen TVs, tea and coffee-making facilities, and daily housekeeping. Some luxury hotels include extras like on-site restaurants, fitness centres, and spa services.

Booking: It is best to reserve your hotel ahead of time, especially during peak tourist seasons. Booking websites and hotel companies provide easy-to-use online reservation systems.

B&Bs (bed and breakfasts)

Bed and breakfasts in Belgium provide a comfortable and personalised accommodation experience. These are frequently located in local houses, and visitors may expect the following:

B&B hosts are well-known for their warm and pleasant welcome. Staying at a bed and breakfast allows you to interact with locals and learn about the area.

B&B accommodations are often more intimate and offer a homey atmosphere. They might feature social rooms as well as gardens for relaxation.

Local food: Some B&Bs serve prepared breakfasts with local delicacies, allowing guests to sample Belgian food.

While B&Bs are not as standardised as hotels, you may expect nice rooms with basic facilities. Because each B&B is unique, it's best to check individual listings for specific options.

Many B&Bs are located in stunning rural locations, making for a calm and gorgeous environment for a relaxing stay.

Alternative Accommodations and Hostels

Hostels and alternative lodgings in Belgium are excellent choices for budget-conscious travellers and those seeking a more sociable atmosphere.

Hostels: Hostels provide inexpensive dormitory-style accommodations as well as individual room alternatives. They are ideal for solitary travellers, backpackers, and anyone looking to meet other adventurers.

Couchsurfing is a network that links travellers with local hosts who offer free lodging. It's a great opportunity to learn about the culture and meet new people.

Guesthouses: Guesthouses, which are generally managed by families, offer inexpensive and comfortable lodging. In comparison to larger hotels, they provide a more personalised experience.

Farm Stays: The countryside of Belgium is filled with farms that welcome visitors. Farm stays provide an opportunity to experience rural living and frequently include home-cooked meals.

Houseboats: In places like Ghent and Bruges, you may stay on gorgeous houseboats, giving you a one-of-a-kind and unforgettable lodging experience.

Glamping: Glamping, or luxury camping, is a growing trend. It mixes the conveniences of a hotel with the natural beauty. Safari tents, treehouses, and yurts are among the glamping possibilities.

Belgium's wide housing options guarantee that visitors with varying interests and budgets can find a place to stay that meets their needs while taking in the country's beauty and culture.

Chapter 4: City Exploration in Belgium

Belgium is home to a multitude of dynamic and picturesque cities, each with its own distinct personality and attractions. In this chapter, we begin our tour in Brussels, the capital city. We'll discover must-see attractions, savour gastronomic delicacies, and explore the city's nightlife and entertainment alternatives.

Brussels is the capital of Belgium.

Brussels, the capital of Belgium and the de facto headquarters of the European Union, is a city of contrasts. It combines a rich historical tapestry with modernism and a cosmopolitan environment with ease. Here are some must-see sights in Brussels:

Must-See Places:

The Grand Place (Grote Markt) is Brussels' major plaza and a beautiful exhibition of Gothic and Baroque architecture. Among the magnificent structures that surround the plaza are the Town Hall and the King's House (Maison du Roi).

Atomium: A symbol of postwar Brussels, this landmark skyscraper was supposed to resemble an iron crystal amplified 165 billion times. Its inside may be explored, which contains exhibitions, a restaurant, and panoramic views.

Manneken Pis: A popular Brussels landmark, this bronze monument of a little boy peeing into a fountain is both amusing and charming. The statue has approximately 1,000 costumes and is frequently clothed in different ways.

Cinquantenaire Park: This lovely park has stunning arches, museums, and gardens. It's a great place for a stroll and a picnic.

European Quarter: As the de facto headquarters of the European Union, Brussels is home to various EU institutions. Learn about the European Union's history and functions by visiting the European Parliament, the European Commission, and the Parlamentarium.

Delights in the Kitchen:

Belgian Waffles: Enjoy the fluffy and scrumptious Belgian waffles, which are frequently offered with a variety of toppings such as chocolate, strawberries, and whipped cream.

Frites (Fries): Enjoy crispy and savoury Belgian fries with a variety of sauces, including the renowned mayo and Andalouse sauce.

Chocolate: As the world's chocolate capital, Brussels is home to a plethora of chocolatiers. Pralines, truffles, and handmade chocolates will tantalise your taste buds.

Mussels: Steamed mussels with white wine, garlic, and herbs are commonly served with crispy French fries.

Beer: Belgium is well-known for its beer culture, with a diverse selection of distinctive beers. Don't pass up the chance to sample some of Belgium's greatest beers, including Trappist ales and lambics.

Entertainment and nightlife:

Delirium Café: According to Guinness World Records, this pub has the most comprehensive beer selection, with over 2,000 types. It's a beer lover's delight.

Art Nouveau Architecture: Brussels is rich in Art Nouveau architecture. Wander around the Ixelles and Schaerbeek neighbourhoods to appreciate the exquisite facades and patterns.

Live Music: The music scene in Brussels is thriving, with various venues holding live events ranging from jazz to modern pop.

Explore the city's street art, featuring comic strip murals that pay homage to Belgium's rich comic book culture.

La Monnaie Opera House: Attend a performance at La Monnaie's Royal Theatre, which is noted for its operas and ballets.

Brussels is an intriguing location for travellers due to its wonderful combination of heritage and innovation. Its historic buildings, excellent cuisine, and active entertainment options make it a memorable city.

Antwerp: The Cultural Centre

Antwerp, Belgium's second-largest city, is renowned as the "City of Diamonds" and is a thriving cultural powerhouse. It is a must-see site due to its rich history, cultural liveliness, and creative legacy. Here, we look at the city's art and culture, as well as its best shopping and the famed Diamond District.

Culture and Art:

The Royal Museum of Fine Arts (Koninklijk Museum voor Schone Kunsten) has a remarkable collection of paintings by Flemish artists such as Rubens, Van Dyck, and Jordaens. It's a veritable treasure trove of Baroque art.

Museum aan de Stroom (MAS): This modern museum on the banks of the River Scheldt provides a unique blend of history, art, and culture. Its rooftop offers a spectacular panoramic view of the city.

Rubenshuis (Rubens House): This museum, which was formerly the home of the famed painter Peter Paul Rubens, gives insight into the artist's life and work. It has a large collection of his artwork and personal items.

Antwerp's Historic Centre: Explore the city's lovely historic centre, complete with cobblestone streets and picturesque squares. The beautiful Cathedral of Our Lady (Onze-Lieve-Vrouwekathedraal), famed for its imposing spire, should not be missed.

Shopping Locations:

Meir: Meir, Antwerp's major shopping street, is a shoppers' paradise. It is lined with foreign and local fashion businesses, as well as some of Belgium's best-known designers.

Antwerp's clothes district: Antwerp is known for its avant-garde clothes and boasts a thriving fashion sector. Explore the fashion district's concept stores, boutiques, and designer shops, as well as the Royal Academy of Fine Arts, where prominent fashion designers learned.

Exquisite Chocolate Stores: Antwerp has a plethora of artisanal chocolate stores. Enjoy pralines, truffles, and other wonderful chocolate treats.

Antique Markets: Visit markets like Vrijdagmarkt and Kloosterstraat to look for one-of-a-kind antiques and vintage items.

The Diamond District

Antwerp is a world-renowned diamond trading centre with an area dedicated to the diamond trade. Visit the Diamond District to browse jewellery stores, observe diamond cutters at work, and learn about the city's diamond heritage.

Diamondland: Located in the Diamond District, this tourist centre gives information on the diamond-cutting process as well as the global diamond trade. It's a chance to gaze at gorgeous diamond jewellery.

Diamond Museums: Visit museums such as DIVA, Antwerp's Diamond Museum, to learn about the world of diamonds. Learn more about the history and workmanship of these exquisite jewels.

Bruges: A Mediaeval Jewel

Bruges, located just a short distance from Antwerp, is a mediaeval marvel that grabs the hearts of those who visit. Its well-preserved mediaeval centre, UNESCO World Heritage designation, and picturesque canals contribute to the city's enthralling aura.

Climb to the top of Bruges' renowned bell tower for panoramic views of the city. The Belfry is an icon of Bruges and provides an amazing sight of the city's mediaeval architecture.

Canal Cruises: Take a canal tour to see Bruges from a fresh viewpoint. The city's gorgeous canals snake through it, providing peaceful vistas of old structures.

Market plaza (Markt) in Bruges: This lively plaza is surrounded by ancient buildings and is a great place to start exploring the city. It's also a fantastic spot for alfresco eating.

Visit the Basilica of the Holy Blood (Heilig-Bloedbasiliek) to see a cherished relic, a phial thought to contain a drop of Christ's blood.

Chocolate and Beer: Bruges, like the rest of Belgium, is famous for its chocolate and beer. Explore local breweries and sample fine chocolates.

Antwerp and Bruges provide an intriguing blend of creative expression and mediaeval beauty. Both towns offer distinct and fascinating experiences, from Antwerp's thriving art scene to Bruges' charming alleyways and canals.

Old Town Historic District:

The ancient old town of Ghent is a mesmerising mix of mediaeval buildings, cobblestone lanes, and gorgeous canals. Here are some highlights to look into:

Gravensteen Castle: Dominating the horizon with its magnificent towers and stone walls, this 12th-century castle gives a look into mediaeval life. You may tour the inside of the castle and climb the battlements for panoramic views.

St. Bavo's Cathedral (Sint-Baafskathedraal): This Gothic architectural marvel houses the famed Ghent Altarpiece. The altarpiece is a masterpiece by the Van Eyck brothers.

Ghent is known as the "City of Three Towers" because of the distinctive trio of St. Nicholas' Church, the Belfry of Ghent, and St. Bavo's Cathedral. These structures command the city's skyline.

Graslei and Korenlei: These gorgeous quaysides along the River Lys are dotted with antique guildhalls and provide an excellent photographic opportunity. They're extremely beautiful when illuminated at night.

Boat Tours and Canals:

Canal Cruises: The canals of Ghent are an important aspect of the city's beauty. A canal trip allows you to see the city from a different angle and admire the ancient structures that border the rivers.

The Leie River flows through Ghent, and its banks are great for strolls or picnics. You may also rent a small boat and paddle along the river on your own.

Waffles and chocolates:

Ghent has some wonderful chocolate stores where you may indulge in pralines, truffles, and chocolate creations. Belgian chocolate is famous for its flavour and quality.

Waffles: Enjoy delicious Belgian waffles from street sellers and cafes across the city. They can be topped with a variety of ingredients, including whipped cream, chocolate, and fresh fruit.

Ghent: A Combination of History and Modernity

Ghent combines its rich past with modernity to create a vibrant and dynamic city.

Ghent is well-known for its lively street art culture. Colourful murals and graffiti decorate the city's walls and facades, providing a contemporary creative touch to its historic setting.

Graffiti Street (Werregarenstraat): A constantly changing canvas for graffiti artists. Anyone interested in urban art should pay it a visit.

Ghent institution: Ghent University is a famous Belgian institution noted for its research and innovation. The college area gives the city a youthful and dynamic vibe.

Cultural Events: Throughout the year, Ghent offers a variety of cultural events and festivals, ranging from music and film festivals to art exhibitions. Check the local events calendar to see if there are any that will overlap with your stay.

Ghent has a diversified culinary scene, with restaurants serving everything from traditional Belgian cuisine to cosmopolitan flavours. Waterzooi (a creamy stew) and Gentse neuzen (cuberdon sweets) are popular local foods.

Ghent's unique combination of history, culture, and contemporary design provides a welcoming atmosphere. Ghent provides a well-rounded and engaging travel experience, whether you're exploring its mediaeval alleyways, enjoying modern art, or savouring Belgian delights.

Architectural Wonders:

Ghent is a veritable treasure trove of architectural wonders spanning decades and styles. Here are some of the most prominent architectural highlights in the city:

St. Bavo's Cathedral (Sint-Baafskathedraal): Ghent's rich history is reflected in this splendid Gothic cathedral. Inside, you may see the world-famous Ghent Altarpiece, a Van Eyck Brothers masterwork.

Gravensteen Castle, which dominates the cityscape, is a mediaeval fortification with towering towers and stone walls. The castle depicts mediaeval life and includes a weapons museum.

The Belfry of Ghent: This 91-metre-tall UNESCO World Heritage monument gives panoramic views of the city. It is an icon of Ghent due to its outstanding construction and chimes.

St. Nicholas' Church, the Belfry, and St. Bavo's Cathedral are known together as "Ghent's Three Towers" and are iconic emblems of the city. Their distinctive architecture and historical significance are must-see attractions.

St. Michael's Bridge (Sint-Michaelsbrug): This bridge provides beautiful views of the city's canals and old buildings, making it a popular photo location.

Mediaeval Guildhalls: Along the Graslei and Korenlei quaysides, you'll discover magnificently restored Middle Ages guildhalls. They add to Ghent's ageless allure.

Cafes and restaurants:

Ghent's food scene is diversified and caters to all tastes. Here are some must-try eating and café experiences:

Cuberdon: Try the local specialty "Gentse neuzen" or cuberdon candy. These raspberry-flavoured cone-shaped candies are a lovely treat.

Waffles: Enjoy traditional Belgian waffles with a variety of toppings such as chocolate, fruit, and whipped cream.

Waterzooi: Don't leave Ghent without trying the creamy Belgian stew Waterzooi, which is often cooked with chicken or fish. It's a regional delicacy.

Restaurants in Ghent: Ghent has a wide range of eating alternatives, from traditional Belgian cuisine to foreign flavours. Discover local eateries and savour Belgian classics.

Cafes: The city's cafes are welcoming locations to unwind with a coffee, a Belgian beer, or a small meal. The café culture of Ghent is an important aspect of the city's vibe.

Ghent Festivals:

Throughout the year, Ghent comes alive with different celebrations and events. Here are some of the city's most well-known festivals:

Gentse Feesten (Ghent Festival): This ten-day festival, held in July, is one of Europe's largest and most dynamic cultural festivals. It includes music, theatre, street acts, and vibrant celebrations all across town.

Ghent's Light Festival is a spectacular festival that fills the city with light art. Every three years, Ghent is transformed into a wonderful wonderland.

Ghent Jazz Festival: Jazz fans will enjoy the Ghent Jazz Festival, which features world-class jazz performers and artists in a variety of historic settings.

Film Fest Gent: This prominent film festival, which features a broad variety of foreign and Belgian films, is a must-see for film enthusiasts. It's a major cultural event on the city's calendar.

Floralies Gent (Ghent Floralies): Every five years, the Floralies Gent show stunning flower and plant displays. Ghent is transformed into a flowery wonderland throughout the festival.

The celebrations in Ghent provide a rich cultural experience as well as the opportunity to rejoice with locals and fellow travellers. Ghent offers a broad and interesting experience for all visitors, whether they are eating gastronomic pleasures, admiring architectural treasures, or participating in exciting events.

Chapter 5: Beyond the Cities

The appeal of Belgium extends far beyond its busy cities. In this chapter, we travel to the wonderful Belgian countryside, where we will experience the Ardennes adventure, picturesque villages, and the splendour of hiking and natural reserves.

Countryside in Belgium:

The Belgian countryside, with its tranquil landscapes and breathtaking panoramas, is a haven of natural beauty and outdoor adventure. Here are a few highlights:

Adventure in the Ardennes:

The Ardennes: The Ardennes, located in southern Belgium, is a natural paradise famed for its rolling hills, lush woods, and flowing rivers. It's a haven for outdoor enthusiasts and thrill-seekers.

Hiking, mountain biking, kayaking, and rock climbing are just a few of the outdoor activities available in the Ardennes. It's a terrific spot to get back in touch with nature and enjoy the great outdoors.

Woods and animals: The dense Ardennes woods are home to a diverse range of animals, including deer, wild boar, and several bird species. Nature enthusiasts will appreciate the peace and opportunities to view animals.

Beautiful Villages:

Durbuy, known as the "Smallest Town in the World," is a lovely town tucked beside the Ourthe River. Its cobblestone alleys, mediaeval buildings, and boutique stores make it a charming destination to visit.

La Roche-en-Ardenne: This lovely village is surrounded by the natural splendour of the Ardennes. Explore its hilltop castle and wander along the Ourthe River's banks.

Dinant is a bustling Meuse River town known for its beautiful citadel and the Collegiate Church of Notre-Dame. It is well-known for its saxophone legacy and gorgeous setting.

Rochefort is a tranquil hamlet famed for its Trappist brewery, which makes well-known Belgian beers. Visit Saint-Remy Abbey and the Lorette Caves.

Nature Reserves and Hiking:

The High Fens (Hautes Fagnes): This Ardennes nature reserve is known for its distinctive peat bog environment. Hikers can uncover uncommon plant species while exploring wooden boardwalks and twisting pathways.

Hoge Kempen National Park: Hoge Kempen, Belgium's only national park, features a broad range of landforms, from heathlands to pine forests. It is ideal for hiking, cycling, and wildlife viewing.

Zwin Nature Park: Zwin Nature Park, located on the North Sea shore, is a sanctuary for migrating birds. It's a lovely spot for birding and admiring the coastline scenery.

Sonian woodland (Forêt de Soignes): This large woodland near Brussels is ideal for strolls and picnics. It offers a peaceful respite from the metropolis.

For those seeking natural beauty, outdoor experiences, and the charm of charming communities, the Belgian countryside is a welcome refuge. You'll feel a stronger connection to Belgium's various and compelling landscapes, whether you're hiking in the Ardennes, experiencing mediaeval cities, or immersing yourself in pristine nature reserves.

Belgian Coast:

Belgium's 42 miles of shoreline along the North Sea present a distinct yet equally fascinating element of the nation. In this section, we'll examine the Belgian coast, the seaside retreats it affords, the activities accessible on its sandy sands, and the coastal food that is a feast for the taste buds.

Seaside Escapes:

Ostend (Oostende): As one of the major coastal cities, Ostend features a busy beach promenade, historic sites, and a dynamic cultural environment. It's a popular attraction for both residents and visitors.

Knokke-Heist: This charming coastal town gives a touch of luxury with its upmarket stores, art galleries, and lovely beaches. It's commonly referred to as the "Monaco of the North" due to its rich ambience.

Blankenberge: Blankenberge is noted for its long sandy beach and crowded promenade, which is great for a leisurely stroll. It's a family-friendly location featuring amusement parks and aquatic sports.

De Haan: This picturesque seaside town is distinguished by its Belle Époque architecture and peaceful surroundings. It's a perfect setting for a tranquil coastal escape.

Beach Activities:

Sunbathing and Swimming: The Belgian coast's broad sandy beaches are great for sunbathing and swimming throughout the summer months. There are designated swimming areas and lifeguard services.

Water Sports: The North Sea provides chances for water sports such as kite surfing, windsurfing, and sailing. Local rental facilities and institutions provide lessons for beginners.

bike: The coastline region is crisscrossed by bike trails, and you may rent bicycles to explore the stunning scenery and attractive villages.

Beach Volleyball: Many beaches include beach volleyball courts, giving you a fun and sporty way to spend your time by the sea.

Seaside Walks: Take leisurely walks along the beach promenades or along the dunes, enjoying the cool sea wind and magnificent sights.

Coastal Cuisine:

North Sea Seafood: Savour fresh harvests from the North Sea, including mussels, shrimp, and sole. Try the iconic Belgian cuisine, "moules-frites," which consists of mussels cooked in several delectable broths, complemented with crispy French fries.

Beachside Cafes: Enjoy a seaside dinner at one of the beachfront cafes, where you can indulge in seafood platters, local beers, and Belgian waffles with a view of the sea.

Ice Cream: Belgian shore towns are famed for their wonderful ice cream parlors. Treat yourself to a scoop of handmade ice cream while you wander down the seafront.

Fresh Pancakes: Satisfy your sweet taste with fresh Belgian pancakes topped with a variety of toppings, including chocolate, whipped cream, and fruit.

Belgian Beers: Explore the beach pubs and have a Belgian beer while viewing the sunset over the North Sea.

The Belgian coast provides a pleasant and sun-kissed retreat where you can recline on sandy coastlines, indulge in beach sports, and taste excellent coastal food. It's a perfect compliment to Belgium's ancient towns and gorgeous countryside, giving a well-rounded trip experience.

Chapter 6: Food and Drink

Belgium is a gourmet sanctuary that tempts the palette with a complex tapestry of aromas and culinary pleasures. In this chapter, we dig into the world of Belgian food, from the classic Belgian waffles and delectable chocolates to the renowned beer culture and a range of exquisite culinary specialties.

Belgian Gastronomy:

Belgium's gourmet sector is defined by a wonderful combination of French and Dutch influences, producing a unique culinary identity. Here are some highlights:

Belgian Waffles with Chocolate:

Belgian Waffles: Belgian waffles are recognised worldwide for their delicious lightness and fluffy texture. They occur in two primary varieties: Brussels waffles (thin and crisp) and Liège waffles (thick and sweet with pearl sugar). Top them with a plethora of toppings, including whipped cream, chocolate, strawberries, and ice cream.

Chocolate: Belgium is the centre of chocolate artistry. Chocolatiers in places like Brussels, Bruges, and Antwerp produce pralines, truffles, and artisanal chocolates of remarkable quality. Visiting a Belgian chocolate shop is an experience that indulges all the senses.

Beer Culture:

Diverse Beer Varieties: Belgium features a startling diversity of beer varieties, from Trappist beers to lambics and blond ales. Sample classic beers with unique flavour characteristics that are a tribute to Belgium's beer culture.

Trappist Breweries: Belgium is home to many Trappist monks manufacturing beer, notably Orval, Chimay, and Westvleteren. Each Trappist brewery has its own specific recipes and brewing practices.

Beer cafés: Belgian beer culture extends to quaint and historic beer cafés. These are venues where you may sample a range of local beers in genuine and pleasant settings.

Beer Festivals: Belgium holds different beer festivals throughout the year, such as the Zythos Beer Festival and the Brussels Beer Project Festival. These events promote the country's beer tradition and give people the opportunity to experience a wide assortment of beers.

Culinary Delicacies:

Mussels: Belgians are famed for their ability to make steamed mussels in rich broths, generally accompanied by a substantial portion of crispy French fries.

Waterzooi: A classic Belgian cuisine, Waterzooi is a creamy stew cooked with chicken or fish, vegetables, and herbs. It's hearty and savoury.

Carbonade Flamande: This Flemish beef stew is cooked with beer, onions, and brown sugar, resulting in a sweet and delicious flavour that's a genuine comfort dish.

Stoemp: Stoemp is a renowned Belgian meal that blends mashed potatoes with vegetables, commonly eaten alongside sausages or meat. It's both full and healthy.

Flemish Asparagus: When in season, don't miss the opportunity to sample Flemish white asparagus, served with butter sauce or mousseline.

Frites (Fries): Belgian fries, called locally "frites," are a must-try. They are commonly served with a broad assortment of condiments, including the renowned mayo and Andalouse sauce.

Cuberdon: These cone-shaped sweets have a delicious raspberry flavour and a crunchy surface. They are a popular sweet dessert in Belgium.

Belgium's culinary landscape is a celebration of different flavours and decades of culinary mastery. Whether you're savouring a waffle in a lovely café, sampling excellent chocolates in a boutique shop, discovering the depths of Belgian beer culture, or indulging in local specialties, the country's food and drink are sure to create a lasting impact on your taste buds.

Dining Experiences:

Dining in Belgium is not simply a meal; it's an experience that blends culinary skill with a profound respect for great ingredients. Here are some ways to have outstanding dining experiences in Belgium:

Local Restaurants:

Michelin-Starred Restaurants: Belgium features a number of Michelin-starred restaurants that offer excellent dining experiences. From three-star institutions like Hof van Cleve in Kruishoutem to one-star jewels sprinkled around the Netherlands, you may relish inventive and excellent meals made by renowned chefs.

Brasseries: Traditional Belgian brasseries serve classic delicacies like moules-frites, waterzooi, and carbonade flamande. These tiny cafés are great for eating robust Belgian food in a calm ambiance.

Local Friteries: For a casual eating experience, visit a local friterie, where you may savour crispy frites served with a choice of tasty sauces. They're excellent for a fast, delightful bite.

Taverne and Bistros: Taverne and bistros provide a combination of classic and modern Belgian food. They are noted for their pleasant, welcoming ambience and various meals.

Food Markets:

Ghent's Friday Market (Vrijdagmarkt): This lively market in Ghent is an excellent location to enjoy local goods, cheeses, and street cuisine. It's a bustling environment with many stalls and sellers.

Brussels' St. Catherine's Market (Marché Sainte-Catherine): Located in the centre of Brussels, this market provides a range of fresh fish, veggies, and gourmet delicacies. It's also surrounded by seafood restaurants where you may have a seafood feast.

Leuven's Weekend Market (Zaterdagmarkt): Leuven's Saturday market is an excellent place to purchase fresh fruit, bread, and local specialties. It's a vibrant market that's excellent for a morning walk.

Antwerp's Exotic Market (Exotische Markt): If you're in Antwerp, don't miss the Exotic Market, which displays a diversity of exotic delicacies and products. It's a gastronomic journey in itself.

Tasting Tours:

Chocolate Tasting Excursions: Explore the world of Belgian chocolate with guided tasting excursions in places like Bruges, Brussels, and Antwerp. You'll tour chocolate stores, learn about the chocolate-making process, and try a selection of scrumptious pralines and truffles.

Beer tasting excursions: Belgium's rich beer culture is best explored through beer tasting excursions. Join guided tours or make your own beer trail, visiting breweries, beer cafés, and local pubs to sample the broad spectrum of Belgian beers.

Cheese and Wine Excursions: Discover excellent Belgian cheeses and wines through guided excursions. Taste artisanal cheeses like Chimay and abbey brews, and try local wines, especially in the gorgeous vineyards of the Flemish Ardennes.

Culinary Walking Tours: Many towns offer culinary walking tours that take you through food markets, local cafes, and hidden gems to sample regional specialties and gourmet delicacies. These trips give insights into the local cuisine and culture.

Dining experiences in Belgium range from the polished and exquisite to the informal and colourful. Whether you're enjoying a Michelin-starred meal, eating local street food at a market, or participating in guided tasting tours, you'll experience the rich and diverse tastes that distinguish Belgian cuisine.
Dining Experiences:

Dining in Belgium is not simply a meal; it's an experience that blends culinary skill with a profound respect for great ingredients. Here are some ways to have outstanding dining experiences in Belgium:

Local Restaurants:

Michelin-Starred Restaurants: Belgium features a number of Michelin-starred restaurants that offer excellent dining experiences. From three-star institutions like Hof van Cleve in Kruishoutem to one-star jewels sprinkled around the Netherlands, you may relish inventive and excellent meals made by renowned chefs.

Brasseries: Traditional Belgian brasseries serve classic delicacies like moules-frites, waterzooi, and carbonade flamande. These tiny cafés are great for eating robust Belgian food in a calm ambiance.

Local Friteries: For a casual eating experience, visit a local friterie, where you may savour crispy frites served with a choice of tasty sauces. They're excellent for a fast, delightful bite.

Taverne and Bistros: Taverne and bistros provide a combination of classic and modern Belgian food. They are noted for their pleasant, welcoming ambience and various meals.

Food Markets:

Ghent's Friday Market (Vrijdagmarkt): This lively market in Ghent is an excellent location to enjoy local goods, cheeses, and street cuisine. It's a bustling environment with many stalls and sellers.

Brussels' St. Catherine's Market (Marché Sainte-Catherine): Located in the centre of Brussels, this market provides a range of fresh fish, veggies, and gourmet delicacies. It's also surrounded by seafood restaurants where you may have a seafood feast.

Leuven's Weekend Market (Zaterdagmarkt): Leuven's Saturday market is an excellent place to purchase fresh fruit, bread, and local specialties. It's a vibrant market that's excellent for a morning walk.

Antwerp's Exotic Market (Exotische Markt): If you're in Antwerp, don't miss the Exotic Market, which displays a diversity of exotic delicacies and products. It's a gastronomic journey in itself.

Tasting Tours:

Chocolate Tasting Excursions: Explore the world of Belgian chocolate with guided tasting excursions in places like Bruges, Brussels, and Antwerp. You'll tour chocolate stores, learn about the chocolate-making process, and try a selection of scrumptious pralines and truffles.

Beer tasting excursions: Belgium's rich beer culture is best explored through beer tasting excursions. Join guided tours or make your own beer trail, visiting breweries, beer cafés, and local pubs to sample the broad spectrum of Belgian beers.

Cheese and Wine Excursions: Discover excellent Belgian cheeses and wines through guided excursions. Taste artisanal cheeses like Chimay and abbey brews, and try local wines, especially in the gorgeous vineyards of the Flemish Ardennes.

Culinary Walking Tours: Many towns offer culinary walking tours that take you through food markets, local cafes, and hidden gems to sample regional specialties and gourmet delicacies. These trips give insights into the local cuisine and culture.

Dining experiences in Belgium range from the polished and exquisite to the informal and colourful. Whether you're enjoying a Michelin-starred meal, eating local street food at a market, or participating in guided tasting tours, you'll experience the rich and diverse tastes that distinguish Belgian cuisine.

Chapter 7: Practical Information

In this chapter, we'll offer you crucial practical information to guarantee a safe and healthy vacation in Belgium. Here, we'll discuss safety and health advice, including emergency contacts and health measures.

Safety and health tips:

Emergency Contacts:

Emergency Services: In case of any emergency, whether medical, fire, or police-related, call 112. This is the universal emergency number in Belgium.

Medical Assistance: If you require medical assistance, contact the nearest hospital or medical institution. Major cities have hospitals with 24-hour emergency departments.

Pharmacies: Look for the "Apotheek" signage, which identifies pharmacies. They generally include a list of neighbouring pharmacies that are open during non-business hours.

Embassy or Consulate: If you are a foreign tourist and have a severe situation, you can contact your country's embassy or consulate in Belgium for assistance.

Lost or Stolen Items: In case your items are lost or stolen, report the event to the local police station and seek a copy of the report for insurance purposes.

Health Precautions:

Health Insurance: Ensure you have adequate travel insurance that covers medical expenditures, including hospitalisation and emergency repatriation. Check whether your house insurance provides any coverage for overseas travel.

Vaccines: Verify with your healthcare practitioner if you need any specific vaccines or preventative measures before coming to Belgium. Routine immunisations, including measles, mumps, rubella, and influenza, are advised.

Healthcare Facilities: Belgium has an outstanding healthcare system with modern hospitals and well-trained medical personnel. Ensure you have enough health insurance or access to healthcare services while in the country.

Pharmacies: Pharmacies in Belgium, labelled "Apotheek," supply over-the-counter pharmaceuticals and prescription drugs. Be mindful of their operating hours, since not all are open 24/7.

European Health Insurance Card (EHIC): If you are an EU citizen, consider acquiring an EHIC, which can provide you with access to vital healthcare services while in Belgium.

drugs: If you use prescription drugs, carry them in their original packaging and bring a copy of your prescription. Belgium may have distinct brand names for pharmaceuticals; therefore, it's important to bring a list of generic names as well.

Water: Tap water in Belgium is typically safe to drink. However, bottled water is widely accessible if you want it.

Food Safety: Food hygiene regulations in Belgium are strong, and you may comfortably enjoy local food. However, like with any overseas vacation, be wary about ingesting food from recognised restaurants.

Traveller's Diarrhoea: While the danger is relatively minimal in Belgium, traveller's diarrhoea can occur. To prevent it, maintain proper cleanliness, avoid ingesting raw or undercooked food, and drink bottled water if you're concerned.

Insect Protection: In some places, insect repellant may be important, especially during the summer. Consider bringing bug repellant to minimise insect-borne infections.

Belgium is a secure and well-developed nation for tourists, but being prepared is crucial for a smooth and pleasurable stay. By knowing the emergency contacts, comprehending health precautions, and having sufficient insurance coverage, you may visit this wonderful place with confidence and peace of mind.

Local Etiquette:
Understanding and following local etiquette is vital when visiting Belgium. Here are some crucial considerations to bear in mind:

Tipping Practices:

Restaurants: Tipping at restaurants is common, but it's not as high as in some other countries. A normal practice is to leave a tip of roughly 10% of the cost, or you can round up the bill if you're happy with the service. In rare situations, a service fee may be included in the bill, so verify before tipping.

Cafes and Bars: Tipping in cafes and bars is not compulsory, although it's appreciated. You can leave a tiny change or round up the bill to the nearest euro.

Taxis: In taxis, it's normal to round up the fare to the nearest euro or give a modest tip for the driver.

Hotels: Tipping hotel workers, including bellhops and housekeeping, is a good gesture, but it's not necessary. You can leave a few euros for the service.

Cultural Norms:

timeliness: Belgians emphasise timeliness; therefore, it's crucial to appear on time for appointments, meetings, and social occasions.

Respect Personal Space: Belgians enjoy personal space and tend to keep a comfortable physical distance during interactions. Be careful of this cultural norm.

Greetings: A typical greeting in Belgium is a handshake. In Flemish-speaking regions, a kiss on both cheeks may be typical among friends, but in Wallonia, a single kiss is normal.

Table Manners: While dining, practice traditional European table manners. Keep your hands on the table, wrists on the edge, and elbows off the table. Wait for the host to begin the dinner before you start eating.

Language: Belgians speak many languages, including Dutch (Flemish), French, and German. Knowing a few simple phrases in the local language might be welcomed; however, many Belgians are fluent in English.

Packing Essentials:

Weather-appropriate clothing: Check the weather forecast for your vacation dates and prepare appropriately. Belgium has a marine environment with fluctuating weather, so layers are typically a smart choice.

Comfortable Shoes: Belgium's cities and towns are frequently best visited on foot, so comfortable walking shoes are important.

Adapters & Converters: Belgium utilises Type E power outlets. If your gadgets have a different plug type, carry the appropriate adapters and voltage converters.

Travel adaptors: Check if your electrical gadgets are compatible with Belgian power outlets, which use Type E connections. If needed, bring plug adapters or voltage converters.

Travel Insurance: It's important to get travel insurance that covers medical expenditures, vacation cancellations, and lost or stolen possessions.

Guidebook: A guidebook or travel app can be helpful for exploring and learning about Belgium's sights and culture.

Local Currency: While ATMs are generally available, it's a good idea to bring some euros with you for little cost upon arrival.

Local SIM Card: If you wish to have access to a local phone number and data, consider obtaining a local SIM card, accessible at the airport or stores.

By sticking to local etiquette, being aware of tipping traditions and cultural norms, and bringing the basics based on the season and your travel needs, you can enrich your experience in Belgium and make the most of your visit to this interesting nation.

What to pack:

Belgium's temperature may be varied, so preparing adequately for your vacation is vital. Here's a guide on what to pack:

Clothing:

Weather-appropriate attire: Bring attire suited for the season. In summer, light and breathable materials are great, while in winter, carry warm layers and a waterproof jacket.

Comfortable Walking Shoes: Belgium's cities and towns are best experienced on foot, so comfortable and supportive walking shoes are a requirement.

Umbrella and Raincoat: Given Belgium's regular rain, owning an umbrella and a lightweight, waterproof raincoat is a wise decision.

Swimsuit: If you want to visit seaside towns or enjoy hotel pools, don't forget to take a swimsuit.

Electronics:

Plug Adapters: Belgium uses Type E power outlets. Ensure you have the proper plug adapters or voltage converters for your gadgets.

Chargers and Power Banks: Don't forget to pack chargers for your electrical gadgets, and consider carrying a power bank for on-the-go charging.

Camera: Capture the beauty of Belgium with a camera or smartphone with a good camera.

Travel Accessories:

Travel paperwork: Bring your passport, visa (if necessary), travel insurance paperwork, and a copy of your itinerary.

Money and Cards: Carry some cash in euros for little needs and have your debit or credit card ready for major purchases.

Backpack or Daypack: A small backpack or daypack might be convenient for transporting essentials when exploring.

Travel Pillow with Eye Mask: For pleasant relaxation during lengthy flights

Travel Lock: To secure your luggage

Toiletries:

Travel-sized amenities: Consider travel-sized amenities, including shampoo, conditioner, body wash, and toothpaste, to conserve room in your luggage.

prescriptions: Pack any necessary prescriptions and a small first-aid kit with necessities like band-aids and pain killers.

Miscellaneous:

Guidebook or Travel App: For travelling and learning about Belgium's sights and culture.

Reusable Water Bottle: Belgium provides clean tap water, so owning a reusable water bottle may save you money and decrease plastic waste.

Adapters: Bring European plug adapters (Type E) for your electrical gadgets.

Sunglasses and sunscreen are especially important during the warmer months.

Travel Gear Recommendations:

Lightweight baggage: Opt for lightweight and robust baggage to make travelling more bearable.

Travel Backpack: A multipurpose travel backpack might be a terrific alternative to standard luggage, especially for individuals who intend to move around frequently.

Packing Cubes: These help keep your things arranged and make packing and unpacking more convenient.

Travel Pillow: A comfy travel pillow may make a great difference during lengthy flights or train excursions.

RFID Blocking Wallet: Protect your passport and cards against digital theft with an RFID-blocking wallet.

Travel Adapter and Voltage Converter: Ensure your electronics can charged and used in Belgian power outlets.

Universal Charger: A universal charger with numerous USB ports may be convenient for keeping gadgets charged.

Travel-Size Toiletry Bottles: Refillable travel-size toiletry bottles are an eco-friendly solution to carry your favourite goods.

Portable Power Bank: Keep your electronics charged on the road with a portable power bank.

Travel Guidebook or App: A guidebook or travel app may give essential information on the finest sites to visit, local customs, and practical travel recommendations.

Remember that the particular goods you carry may vary depending on the season and the nature of your vacation. Make sure to check the weather forecast and your schedule to pack properly and make the most of your stay in Belgium.

Chapter 8: Resources and Contacts

In this last chapter, we'll offer you a list of essential contacts that might assist you on your travels in Belgium, including tourist information centres and embassy and consulate data.

Useful Contacts:

Tourist Information Centres:

Visit Flanders: The official tourist board for Flanders, the northern region of Belgium, They give information about places including Brussels, Antwerp, and Bruges. Website: www.visitflanders.com

Wallonia Tourism: The official website for the Wallonia region, including information about places such as Namur, Liège, and Dinant. Website: www.wallonia.be

Brussels Tourism: The official tourism portal for the Brussels-Capital Region Find information on the capital city, including museums, events, and restaurants. Website: visit.brussels

Belgium Tourist: The official tourist website for Belgium gives a thorough description of the country's attractions, activities, and events. Website: www.belgium.be

Tourist Information Centres: Local tourist information centres are placed across Belgium's cities and villages, giving maps, brochures, and guides to help you make the most of your visit.

Embassy and Consulate Details:

If you are a foreign visitor and want assistance from your own country's embassy or consulate, below is the information for some of the important diplomatic missions in Belgium:

Embassy of the United States in Belgium:

Address: Boulevard du Régent 27, 1000 Brussels Phone: +32 2 811 4000
Website: be.usembassy.gov
Embassy of the United Kingdom in Belgium:

Address: Avenue d'Auderghem 10, 1040 Brussels Phone: +32 2 287 6211 Website:

www.gov.uk/world/organisations/british-embassy-brussels

Embassy of Canada in Belgium:

Address: Avenue des Arts 58, 1000 Brussels
Phone: +32 2 741 0611 Website:
www.canadainternational.gc.ca/belgium-belgique/ Embassy of Australia in Belgium:

Address: Avenue des Arts 56, 1000 Brussels
Phone: +32 2 286 0500
Website: belgium.embassy.gov.au Embassy of
India in Belgium:

Address: 217 Chaussee de Vleurgat, 1050
Brussels Phone: +32 2 640 9140 Website:
www.indianembassy.be
Please note that this list covers the contact
information of numerous major embassies and

consulates, but there may be more that are relevant to your native country. Always keep your embassy or consulate's contact information readily available when travelling for any assistance you might require.

With these handy contacts, you may obtain information and services that will enrich your experience and provide support throughout your stay in Belgium. Whether you're seeking direction from tourist information centres or require assistance from your embassy or consulate, these resources are available to help you make the most of your vacation.

Recommended Reading:

To explore more of the history, culture, and different landscapes of Belgium, try adding these books to your reading list:

"The Man Who Spoke Snakish" by Andrus Kivirähk: Although this novel is set in Estonia, it gives intriguing insights into the culture and mythology of the Baltic area, which shares certain connections with Belgium's past.

"In Bruges" by Martin McDonagh: This drama, which inspired the blockbuster film of the same name, portrays the dark humour and peculiar spirit of the city of Bruges.

"The Belgians: An Unexpected Nation" by Stephen W. S. Rendall: Explore the rich history and identity of the Belgian people via this enlightening book.

"A History of Belgium From the Roman Invasion to the Present Day" by Derek Blyth: This comprehensive history book gives a complete grasp of Belgium's past and its effect on the present.

"The Brontës in Brussels" by Helen MacEwan: Delve into the literary history of Brussels, where Charlotte Bront lived and wrote throughout her stay in the city.

Further reading and references:

For additional in-depth information and travel preparation, consider checking the following references and sources:

"Lonely Planet Belgium & Luxembourg": A complete travel guide with specific information on sights, lodgings, and practical travel advice

"Rough Guide to Belgium and Luxembourg": An insightful handbook that gives insights into Belgium's rich culture and history

"DK Eyewitness Travel Guide Belgium and Luxembourg": Packed with magnificent photos, this guide is a visual feast and a wonderful resource for visitors.

Official Tourism Websites: Visit the official tourism websites of Belgium, Flanders, Wallonia, and individual places you wish to explore for the most up-to-date information and travel advice.

Local Books and Websites: Seek out books and websites produced by residents or expats who provide their personal views about Belgian culture, food, and hidden jewels.

Historical and cultural materials: Consult historical and cultural materials to better appreciate Belgium's rich legacy, including books, movies, and academic articles.

By immersing yourself in the recommended reading materials and utilising the resources offered, you may develop a greater awareness of Belgium's past, present, and interesting characteristics that make it a distinctive and welcoming location. These recommendations will improve your vacation experience and help you explore the hidden treasures that Belgium has to offer.

Appendices:

Maps and Navigation:

Navigating Belgium is made simpler with the use of informative maps and guides. Here, you'll find information about several maps and navigation resources to help you discover the cities and areas of Belgium.

City Maps:

City-Specific Maps: Most major Belgian cities, including Brussels, Antwerp, Bruges, and Ghent, give free city maps at tourist information centers. These maps often emphasise significant sites, attractions, and public transportation lines.

Online Mapping Services: Platforms like Google Maps, MapQuest, and Apple Maps offer extensive city maps and navigation features. Download the maps for offline usage or use your mobile data to explore on the fly.

Paper Maps: While digital maps are helpful, consider packing a paper map of the place you're visiting. They can be beneficial when your phone power is low or when you want a practical reference.

Regional Maps:

Regional Tourist Maps: Tourist information centres in Belgium offer regional maps that include various cities and attractions within a defined area. These are ideal for arranging day excursions and visiting the neighbouring regions.

Belgian Railway Network Maps: If you want to travel between cities by train, Belgium's railway network maps are important. They illustrate the railway lines linking different areas and cities, making it easier to organise your travel.

Hiking and Cycling Maps: For outdoor lovers, Belgium provides a wealth of hiking and cycling routes. You may get specific maps and guides for these activities at local bookstores and tourist information centres.

GPS and Navigation Applications: Besides the common map applications listed before, consider utilising navigation apps like Waze or specialist GPS apps for hiking and bicycling if you intend to explore the countryside.

Regional Road Atlases: For those embarking on road travel, a regional road atlas gives a complete picture of the road network and can be helpful for traversing less metropolitan regions.

Remember to examine these maps and navigation materials before and during your journey to Belgium. Whether you're wandering through attractive ancient towns, visiting gorgeous countryside, or enjoying the bustling city life, having the correct maps and navigation tools at your disposal assures a smooth and pleasurable journey.

Glossary of Common Terms:

Here is a list of popular terminology and idioms that may be useful when travelling in Belgium:

Dutch/Flemish: The official language in the northern area of Belgium, Flanders. Dutch is usually referred to as Flemish in Belgium.

French/Walloon: The official language in the southern area of Belgium, Wallonia. French is the prevalent language in this region.

German is the official language in a tiny section of eastern Belgium, near the German border.

Brussels-Capital Zone: The capital of Belgium and the de facto capital of the European Union, a multilingual zone where both Dutch and French are official languages.

Chocolatier: A skilled artisan or establishment specialising in the manufacturing of high-quality chocolate and sweets.

Trappist Beer: A type of beer manufactured by Trappist monks, recognised for its quality and tradition.

Belfry: A tall, mediaeval bell tower present in many Belgian cities, frequently a UNESCO World Heritage site.

Canal Cruise: A popular pastime in places like Bruges and Ghent, offering lovely boat cruises along mediaeval canals

Friterie: A small, local business or stand specialising in Belgian fries (frites) with a variety of toppings and sauces.

Moules-Frites: A typical Belgian meal consisting of mussels served with a side of fries.

Useful Phrases and Translations:

Here are some useful phrases and translations in the three main languages of Belgium:

Dutch/Flemish:
- ★ **Hello - Hallo**
- ★ **Thank you - Dank u wel (formal) / Dank je wel (informal)**
- ★ **Please - Alsjeblieft**
- ★ **Yes - Ja**

★ No - Nee

★ Excuse me - Pardon

★ Good morning - Goedemorgen

★ Good afternoon - Goedemiddag

★ Good evening - Goedenavond

★ Goodbye - Tot ziens

French/Walloon:

★ Hello - Bonjour

★ Thank you - Merci

★ Please - S'il vous plaît (formal) / S'il
   te plaît (informal)

★ Yes - Oui

★ No - Non

★ Excuse me - Excusez-moi (formal) /
   Excuse-moi (informal)

★ Good morning - Bonjour

★ Good afternoon - Bon après-midi

★ Good evening - Bonsoir

★ Goodbye - Au revoir

German:

★ Hello - Hallo

★ Thank you - Danke

★ Please - Bitte

★ Yes - Ja

★ No - Nein

★ Excuse me - Entschuldigen Sie (formal) / Entschuldige (informal)

★ Good morning - Guten Morgen

★ Good afternoon - Guten Tag

★ Good evening - Guten Abend

★ Goodbye - Auf Wiedersehen

Learning and using these basic phrases can greatly enhance your travel experience in Belgium and demonstrate your appreciation for the local culture and language.

Printed in Great Britain
by Amazon

39ca16f1-3e02-4941-aff0-ff8ba403566fR01